# HOW TO SUCCEED IN
# SPORTS
## WITHOUT EVER PLAYING

**Megan Stine
& H. William Stine**

.Illustrated by Howard Cruse

SCHOLASTIC BOOK SERVICES
New York Toronto London Auckland Sydney Tokyo

ISBN 0-590-31997-3

Copyright © 1981 by H. William Stine and Megan Stine.
All rights reserved. Published by Scholastic Book Services, a division of Scholastic Inc.

12 11 10 9 8 7 6 5 4 3 2 1          11          1 2 3 4 5 6/8

Printed in the U.S.A.          01

# TABLE OF CONTENTS

# INTRODUCTION

How many times has this happened to you in phys. ed. class?

The quarterback sends you out for a pass but he sends you to the next state.

Your basketball captain says she's seen head colds that dribble better than you do.

When the rest of the class is doing the shot put, your teacher tells you to do the *stay* put.

You clear the high jump bar at 5'6" and then trip over a small pebble in the dirt.

You open the first page of a book, and it asks a lot of personal questions about your sports ability!

If you answered Yes to any of those questions, *keep reading!* If you always wanted to be an athlete, but you're such a klutz that you can't open a car door one-handed, *keep reading!* If the only roar you hear from the crowd is laughter, *keep reading!*

This book can't make a real athlete out of you. But it can do the next best thing: make other people *think* that you are a real athlete. In other words, this book does what everyone said was impossible — helps you fool *all* the people *all* the time.

Keep reading and learn the right things to say, the right things to do, even the right things to wear so that no one will be able to tell the difference between you and someone who is really good at sports. And remember our motto: It's not whether you win or lose, but whether you look like a winner that counts.

# ★ WHO SHOULD READ THIS BOOK

1. Anyone who is always last to be chosen for teams.
2. Anyone shorter than 6'2" or weighing more than 200 pounds or both.
3. Anyone whose last name begins with X.
4. Anyone who is all thumbs or has two left feet.
5. Anyone who has acquired an embarrassing nickname like Butter Belly, Jello Mold, or Turtle.
6. Anyone who takes notes during roll call.
7. Anyone who schedules dentist appointments to get out of phys. ed.

# ★ WHO SHOULD NOT READ THIS BOOK

1. Anyone who has more than three pictures in the yearbook.
2. Anyone who calls the phys. ed. teacher by his or her first name.

3. Anyone who has been slapped on the bottom more than 25 times since the age of 12.
4. Anyone nicknamed Killer, Cruiser, Crusher, etc.
5. Anyone who still wants to run track in shorts during a snowstorm.
6. Coaches, teachers, or anyone even distantly related to Vince Lombardi.

# ★ TESTIMONIALS

Here is what famous athletes and sports writers are saying about this book even before they read it. Unfortunately, for some unknown reason, none of them would let us use their names.

The reason I know I'm going to love your book as soon as it arrives in the mail is that finally someone is going to tell young people the truth about sports. It's not all glamour and fun. It's hard work followed by hard work and then some more. And I know from just talking to you on the phone, you understand what sports are all about. I'd be proud to have you on my team. In fact, since I was fired, I'd be proud to have anyone on my team. Do you know of any openings for a top-notch pro coach who has recently decided to lighten his schedule a little? I'd even consider a junior high. Am looking forward to receiving your book and the money as we discussed.

*A famous coach*

I really loved this book a lot. I couldn't put it down. Maybe because I put too much stickum on my hands.

*A famous football player*

I thought I knew everything there was to know about playing football. But reading this book was like going back to school for me. I was really glad to know that there's no rule against bringing a radio into the huddle. All the guys love the music and sometimes we even dance. Thanks.

*An even more famous football player*

I picked up a lot of pointers while reading your book. Now what am I going to do with all of these hunting dogs? They have fleas, and my car smells like a kennel.

*A famous tennis pro*

That turkey is not more famous than I am.

*The first famous football player*

I bought your informative book and just two short weeks later, I finished reading it. Now I know I've got what it takes to be a great skier. I wear my ski clothes and parkas every day to school. I eat a lot of Swiss chocolates and even learned how to spell the word *slalom*.

Could you please send me by mail twelve feet of snow?

> *A famous jerk from Mobile, Alabama*

Listen, you tell Mr. Football Hero the only thing that gets sacked more than he does is food in a grocery store.

> *The **still** even more famous football player*

Oh, yeah? Well, the closest you'll ever get to the pigskin is eating sausages for breakfast.

> *A famous football player who will stomp your face if you print another testimonial from that other turkey*

Dear Abby, My husband snores during dinner and — whoops, sorry. I've mailed this letter to the wrong address.

> *A famous wife*

This book is a travesty. Expect to hear from our family lawyers immediately.

> *A distant relative of Vince Lombardi.*

---
★
---

# TEST YOURSELF: HOW MUCH DO YOU KNOW ABOUT SPORTS?

Sure, we've got your money, but how do we know we've got your full attention? The best way is to give a test right after the introduction. That should separate those of you who think this is a big joke from those of you who sincerely believe, as we do, that dreams really do come true . . . if you're sneaky, tricky, and deceitful enough to help them along.

Maybe your dream is a full-page photo of yourself in the yearbook with the caption "Sports Player of the Decade." How are you going to help that dream along if right now you think a three-second violation should be punishable by death? Or you don't know the difference between a right tackle and a right guard? (Of course, you'd learn the difference very quickly if you tried to spray a right tackle under your arm.) Any sports career, even one as dishonest as yours, has to be built on sports basics. So let's just see how many of these basic sports words, rules, and objects you're familiar with.

But don't think of this so much as a test. True, there are questions with wrong and right answers, and you'll be graded on your performance. We'll also make fun of you if you do badly. But think of it as a dentist's exam. We're going to look into your head and where we find a cavity, we'll fill it with sports know-how.

Now, rinse, spit, and take the test. We haven't got all day.

# ★ VERBAL RECOGNITION

1) A sweatband is:
   a) what was left after Blood and Tears left the music business.
   b) useful for keeping hair out of your face, so photographers can see your intense expressions.
   c) Duh, I don't know.

2) What is a full count?
   a) A British nobleman after a large dinner.
   b) The only excitement baseball has to offer.
   c) Duh . . . that's even harder than the last one.

3) A double wing formation is:
   a) a light snack at the Colonel's.
   b) less vulnerable to the blitz.
   c) What's a blitz?

4) What's a blitz?
   a) Something you eat with sour cream and blueberries.
   b) Is this a joke?
   c) If it's a joke, I don't get it.

5) What is a gridiron?
   a) What you use to smooth out a wrinkled grid.
   b) One more stupid question like that, and I refuse to answer.
   c) I think it's like a blitz.

6) What is a full court press?
   a) A dry cleaners across the street from the Hall of Justice.
   b)
   c) Where did the other answer go?

# ★ VISUAL RECOGNITION

1)

This is
a) the fastest way to get a seat on a crowded bus.
b) Mean Joe Green taking a lie detector test.
c) a drunken tic-tac-toe game.

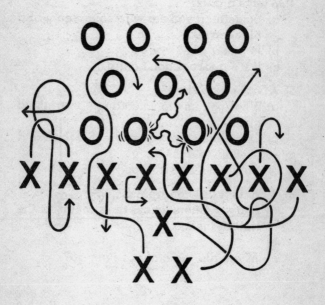

2)

This is

a) the best way for taking attendance on *Eight Is Enough*.

b) a highway mileage sign when you're more than halfway to the people's house you're visiting.

c) unimportant. It's how you play the game that counts.

3)
This is
a) gonna hurt.
b) a cure for chronic nail biting.
c) new regulation equipment for hockey players.

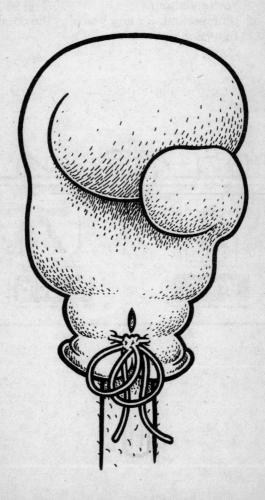

**4)**

This is
a) why your backhand has been a little off today.
b) why there have been so many flies in the house lately.
c) a racket autographed by Ilie Nastase.

5)

This is

a) the letter L.

b) the letter P.

c) the letter you wrote to your uncle last week.

# ★ SCORING

Scoring is a matter of points. And about the only point sharper than the one on your pencil is the one on your head if you think you know enough about sports to fake it — er, uh, make it as an athlete without reading the rest of this book. You probably didn't even know that in football you score six points for crossing the goal line. You also score seven points for tearing across the dotted line, and one point for falling for such an old line.

# ★ WHAT YOUR SCORE MEANS
## Verbal Recognition

If you knew what verbal recognition meant, skip sports and go directly to the S.A.T.'s.

*If you answered letter (a) to most questions:* Skip sports and go directly to student government. You make about as much sense as they do.

*If you answered letter (b) to most questions:* You probably don't want to succeed in sports without even trying at all. In fact, you're probably good at sports. Just as we suspected! You're a spy hired by a distant relative of Vince Lombardi. Drop this book immediately! You heard us: IMMEDIATELY!

*If you answered letter (c) to most questions:* You're just the person who needs this book the most. Your mind is as clean and white as a field of freshly fallen snow — and about as cold and frozen, too. But nothing is impossible — futile maybe, but impossible? Never. We can turn your name into a household word in the sports world. After all, we did it for Morris Burkhart, Carla Erskine, and Beau Tonneau, and we can do it for you. How, you ask, did we change mediocre athletes like Burkhart, Erskine, and Tonneau into household words? By changing their names to Morris Refrigerator, Carla Television, and Beau Stopped-up Sink!

So read on. Sports success is just around the next page!!!

---

Well, what are you looking down here for? You don't think we're actually going to *score* the Visual Recognition test, do you? It's too stupid for words. In fact, that's why it was *pictures!* We told you to read on — and if you want to succeed at sports, you're going to have to learn to do what your coach tells you. So get going! Go on! Hurry up. Bye Bye!

---

# ★
# THE OBJECT
# OF THE GAME

The sports world is beginning to suffer from an overpopulation problem of its own. It almost seems as though new and unusual sports are being invented at the drop of a hat. Hey! Maybe there's a new sport in that!

We don't want you to feel lost in the shuffle. After all, how can you succeed at sports you've not only never played, but have no idea what's going on when other people are playing them? You've got to look as though you're familiar with every bunt, punt, slap, and jump shot there is, and you don't have time to do a lot of studying. To help you ease your way into any sports conversation, the following pages will tell you everything you need to know about every important sport known to man and woman at the present time. And remember:

Don't feel bad about giving opinions about sports you've never played. Sportswriters do it all the time.

## KICKBALL

This sport is essentially identical to baseball except a basketball or soccer ball is thrown by the pitcher and *kicked* by the "batter." It's usually played in school where coaches are afraid to hand out wooden bats to students.

## DODGEBALL

The object of this game doesn't seem to be much more than throwing a large ball at someone and trying to hit them on the legs, chest, or face and leave a large, red welt. The game can be confusing because it's exactly what you were told not to do as a child.

## TENNIS

This is a sport where you can really show your stuff — your designer tennis clothes, designer shoes, designer rackets, and designer haircuts. The object of the game is to blind your opponents by being tall, blond, and wearing all white.

## DIVING

People jump off a diving board twenty-five feet above a swimming pool and then try to do everything they can not to hit the water. Nobody ever wins in this sport.

## ICE HOCKEY

This game is the exact duplicate of soccer, except instead of being played on a grass or indoor field, it's played on an ice rink. Instead of wearing track shoes, players wear ice skates. Instead of kicking a large, soft ball, they strike a small, hard puck with long sticks, not their feet. And instead of thin shorts and shirt, players wear heavy clothing with thick padding. But other than that, the games are the same. Players can be taken off the ice to spend time in a "penalty box" for unsportsmanlike conduct, such as not fighting or delaying the game. A slap shot is what you get when you try to pick up the team captain's girlfriend in the stands.

## BASEBALL (simple explanation)

Stand out in the hot sun for three hours and try to remember to look up in the sky when someone finally hits the ball. When you're at bat, try to find the ball coming at you in a ninety-mile-an-hour pitch.

## BASEBALL (complicated explanation)

Often called the All-American game, probably because the players go out on strike as often as they are called out on strikes. Two teams of nine players (don't ask about the designated hitter rule, just don't ask) play each other for nine innings. The game would have been even more complicated if the men who invented it could have counted past nine.

When a team is on defense, it's called "taking the field." When the other team is on offense, it's called "being at bat." When both teams are on the field, it's called a fistfight. The pitcher (not pronounced *picture*) tries to throw the ball past the batter. The batter swings a wooden stick at the ball. If the batter hits the ball with the stick, it's called a hit. If the batter misses the ball, he probably won't be asked to make many commercials. If the pitcher hits the batter with the ball, it's called an accident. If the pitcher hits the batter with the ball twice, it's called a coincidence. If the pitcher hits the batter with the ball three times, it's called target practice, and it usually brings both teams out on the field at the same time, and we know what that's called. Pitchers can be sent to the showers, usually because they stink. Batters are just sent to the Minors.

## FOOTBALL

Thirty-three hundred pounds in blue uniforms smash into thirty-three hundred pounds in red uniforms. Whoever comes up breathing carries the ball.

## VOLLEYBALL

This game was invented for people who fall down a lot and want to look heroic doing it. It's interesting to note that the game was invented exactly one week after the discovery of the floorburn. After the discovery of the grass stain and sand-burn, the game was moved to lawns and beaches. The game is popular mostly with people on soft-drink commercials.

## JAI ALAI

There is no object to this game. How can there be an object to a game that no one even knows how to pronounce?

## JAVELIN THROW

No one knows anything about this sport, since spectators are too afraid for their lives to be anywhere around when it's happening.

## DISCUS

The object here is to throw a discus — a flat, hard plate — as far as you can. The sport has been ruined by certain environmentalists who insist on using recyclable paper plates.

## ROLLER DISCUS

Bright lights, loud music, roller skates, and crazy clothes have been added to this event to attract more participants to what is an otherwise ridiculous sport.

## SHOT PUT

How far can you throw a thirty-pound, solid metal ball?

## SHOT PUTT

How far can you putt a thirty-pound, solid metal ball?

## SHOTTT PUTTT

This is a typographical error.

## SLALOM

A downhill race on skis around obstacles in the snow — usually the racers who went before you.

## SQUASH, PADDLE BALL, RACQUET BALL

The same dumb game, only the price bracket changes.

## BASKETBALL

One of the highest-scoring games and no wonder. You get two points per basket unless you get three. You get one point for a free throw unless you get two chances to make one point or three chances to make two. You also get a calculator when you join the team. Basketball is a lot like doing laps in a swimming pool without the water to cool you off.

## GOLF

Often called the All-American game by people who hate baseball. Players — the ones wearing the ugly, bright shirts (the spectators wear ugly, bright shirts and ugly, bright hats) — try to hit a small ball over the entire length of the course in as few strokes as possible, unless they have one massive coronary out of sheer frustration. To hit the ball, players use different kinds of clubs: the putter, for short shots; irons, for long shots; woods — this is where the ball usually ends up.

# FENCING

This is an illegal activity, and we can't discuss it in this book.

# CONTRACT BRIDGE

This is a game of chance, when you happen to call someone from the underworld a dummy, and they put out a contract on your life.

# CONTACT BRIDGE

A game involving a deck of cards and four very hotheaded players. The game seldom advances beyond one hand of cards before arguments break out that inevitably lead to fistfights and brawls.

# SOCCER

You're probably waiting for us to make some joke about soccer being one sport where the players really use their heads. Forget it. We wouldn't take a cheap shot like that. After all, soccer players face severe adversity. For instance, they can never wear sunglasses because their faces are flat as pancakes and the glasses slide off their noses.

# ★
# DRESSING LIKE AN ATHLETE

What makes an athlete stand out in a crowd, while you just stand out in the rain? Their size? Their grace? Their sly wit and humor? Get serious! You can always tell athletes because they look like athletes. That means they dress like athletes, in a unique style of fashion that comes from staring too hard at bubble gum cards.

If you want people to think you're an athlete, you're going to have to learn how to dress like one. Fortunately for you, all of this is spelled out in fascinating detail on the next several pages. So all you have to do is select a look that fits, at a price that fits.

There are two basic athletic looks to strive

for — the basic all-around athlete and the basic jock. The basic all-around athlete or sporty person runs, jogs, plays tennis, rides anything with four legs, and attends every social event wearing some reminder of his or her physical fitness addiction: a towel around the neck, running shoes even at the prom. Why go into details when you *know* the type? This person is already at least halfway clued in to the philosophy behind this book because he knows that *appearances count.* You've never seen most of these show-offs anywhere near a tennis court, have you? Yet the perennial tennis racket glued to our basic athlete's hand convinces you that he is aces on the court. Well, guess what? You, too, can take advantage of the power of positive appearances. People won't care if you're rotten at sports if you're rich enough to keep up sports appearances.

On the other hand, maybe you fancy looking like a jock. But if you do, don't use the word "fancy" in the locker room or you'll be thrown out of there on your ever-so-often-slapped behind. The jock look is almost harder to cultivate because jocks don't care what they wear as long as it looks good with blood on it.

In case either the "Basic Athlete" or the "Basic Jock" look is too expensive for your pocketbook, we've provided Do-It-Yourself versions of each. By the use of clever, almost imperceptible substitutions you can pass yourself off as being at the height of fashion while you're in the depths of poverty.

# ★ BASIC ATHLETE

- Designer jogging suits in six colors so you can change colors between every class.

- Combination tank watch, stopwatch, chronometer, pedometer, thermo-indicator, and snooze alarm. It's so heavy you could never play any sport wearing it, but at $750 a throw, who'd want to?

- Sweatbands on *everything* — forehead, wrists, ankles, knees, upper arms, elbows, thighs, neck, waist, and pinkies — every place but under your arms where you really need them!

- Running shoes with built-in "Foot Fone" radio, so you can enjoy life in the fast lane and get the traffic reports at the same time. Leaves your hands free to keep those idiotic earphones from bouncing off your head while you run.

- Socks with the price tag still attached because otherwise you can't tell the difference between cheap, white athletic socks and designer, white athletic socks.

- Belted ice bucket for carrying expensive bottled water while you run.

- Prescription sun visor that changes from clear glass indoors to dark gray outdoors, so you never have to take it off. Assures that people know you're an athlete even in movie theaters, restaurants, etc.

- Swiss Army Sports Tool — has nine pieces of upperclass sports equipment in one: tennis racket, squash paddle, billiard cue, polo mallet, golf club, handball glove, croquet mallet, riding crop, and cricket wicket.

# ★ DO-IT-YOURSELF ATHLETE

- White jogging suit and six boxes of dye in progressively darker colors. Can still change colors between each class but wet dye comes off on your skin.

- No money for expensive watch — carry lots of dimes and call for the time whenever you want.

- Sweatbands made out of socks: two socks tied together for your forehead, one sock tied around each wrist.

- Running shoes — save a little money by buying the off-brands like Adodos, Puka, Toetorn, and Kuds. From a distance no one will be able to tell the difference as you go running by.

- Socks — no socks; you're wearing both of your pairs on your wrists and forehead.

- Sun visor — cut the top out of an old baseball cap.

- Girl or Boy Scout folding cup for borrowing expensive bottled water from Basic Athlete.

- Equipment — you can't afford a tennis

racket, etc., so carry lots of tennis balls instead.

- Table radio for listening to sounds while running.

- Fifteen-mile extension cord for radio.

# ★ BASIC JOCK

- Gray athletic T-shirt must be grimy, torn, and cut off at the waist to expose the belly button. Take it off frequently and use it to mop your sweaty "bod" to achieve the proper odor.

- Blue jeans must be grimy, torn, and cut off at the waist to expose the belly button. Take them off frequently and use them to mop the floor to achieve the proper color.

- Sweat socks must be grimy, torn, and cut off at the waist to expose the belly button. Don't ever take them off to achieve the appropriately disgusting odor.

- Grimy, torn tennis shoes can be taken off if you want, but with those socks, just remember how many friends you could lose.

### Jock Sports Equipment

- As everyone knows, jocks don't carry around equipment. So the only thing you'll need is an empty soda can to smash against your forehead. Of course, *true* jocks use *full* soda cans. It's up to you.

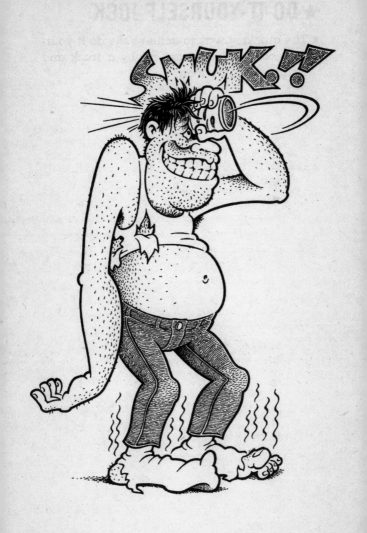

# ★ DO-IT-YOURSELF JOCK

- The quickest way to achieve the do-it-your-self jock look is to get hit by a truck and dragged twenty feet.

# ★
# TALKING THE LANGUAGE

Now that you've learned how to look like an athlete, you need to learn how to talk a good game, too, because there's more to seeming like an athlete than meets the eye. Face it: You'll never be convincing as a sports fanatic if you keep saying things such as, "Why don't they all take turns being quarterback?"; "Who's Vince Lombardi?"; and things like that.

To demonstrate just how utterly essential it is to talk like a jock, we are about to submit you to "The Blindfold Test." However, we don't recommend really wearing a blindfold because then you wouldn't be able to read the book.

Imagine this typical situation you probably find yourself in twice a week at least. You are at a school pep rally, and you are blindfolded and can't see a thing. Two people step to the microphone. Can you tell which one is the athlete?

Person #1 clears his throat loudly into the microphone and then says, "Gosh, guys and gals. We're going to try pretty hard to play a good game and not get our uniforms dirty. Remember, it's not whether you win or lose that counts. It's something else, although I can't remember what it is right now. But, gee, thanks for coming anyway."

Person #2 steps to the microphone and tears it apart with his bare hands. Then he bellows so loud it registers on the Richter scale, "Shut up! I'm talking!" This not only stops all the talking in the auditorium, but some of the breathing as well. Then he says, "There won't be enough left of their team to send home in an envelope!" The crowd goes berserk with applause and cheers.

Now, if you thought Person #1 sounded the most like an athlete, you'd better start re-reading this book, beginning with the cover. But don't be discouraged. No one said this was going to be easy. Tell yourself you really have what it takes. You can be lazy. You can let others do the work while you take the credit. You can make people think you're a sports star. Now start the book over; we'll wait for you right here.

If, however, you wisely perceived that Person #2 in "The Blindfold Test" sounded most like an athlete, you're right. And, in fact, that speech was actually given by Collin Allcars, captain of the Tacoma High School chess team. The team has won every game by default because their opponents were too afraid of Collin to get off the bus. Collin memorized this book from cover to cover, and someday he even hopes to learn how to play chess, but there's no hurry. Collin has already been offered chess scholarships from three different universities.

The point is that Collin has learned what you are about to learn — how to talk like an athlete. The next chapter, "Understanding the Jocks," will focus on what the *real* athletes mean by what they say; but this chapter will concentrate on when and how *you* can sound like an athlete and to whom.

**TALKING THE LANGUAGE RULE #1:** *There's nothing more important to an athlete than sports.*

This means you will have to drop certain topics from your conversation. They are:

World Events
Politics
The Economy
Nuclear Energy
Movies
Television
Dating
Fashion
Computer Programming

The Effects of Daylight Savings Time on the
  Fiscal Year
Japanese Haiku Poetry
Do Bears Dream During Hibernation?
Ecology
Pop Music
The Humanities
The Inhumanities
Insecticides (which are not bugs committing
  suicide)
Red China
Yellow Journalism
Brown Paper Packages Tied Up With String
All of Your Favorite Things

**TALKING THE LANGUAGE RULE #2:** *Be totally self-absorbed.*

If athletes were any more self-absorbed, they'd be rolls of paper towel. What this means for you is simply this: From now on, if you want to sound like an athlete, you will have two topics of conversation: 1) how I played in the last big game; and 2) how I am going to play in the next big game.

**TALKING THE LANGUAGE RULE #3:** *Act as though everyone is as interested in sports as you are.*

Tell yourself that there is no one too important, too dumb, too busy, or too dead to listen to you talk about: 1) how you played in the last big game; and 2) how you are going to play in the next big game.

If you're still a little confused, just follow the following examples.

**Talking the Language in Class:**

TEACHER: Students, George Washington once threw a dollar across the Potomac River.

YOU: Last week I made a 25-foot standing broad jump.

TEACHER: Who won the French-Indian War?

YOU: I don't know, but it should have been Cleveland. They have some great pitching talent.

TEACHER: How would you bisect an equilateral triangle?

YOU: I'd use a blitzing linebacker.

TEACHER: What do they call it when the king of one country marries the queen of another country?.

YOU: A heavyweight title match.

**Talking the Language on a Date:**

YOUR DATE: How did you like the movie?

YOU: I thought the best part was when I sprinted around left end, got underneath the zone interference, and went all the way to the popcorn stand and back without being touched.

YOUR DATE: Let's go get something to eat.

YOU: I know a great place where we can get raw liver and milkshakes to build up my blood.

YOUR DATE: What's your sign?

YOU: If the third-base coach touches his

cap, that means don't swing; if he wipes his forehead, that means bunt; if he blows his nose, that means he has a cold.

**Talking the Language at Home:**

YOUR MOTHER: Take out the trash.

YOU: Sorry, Mom, I've got to go to practice now.

YOUR FATHER: Wash the dishes.

YOU: Sorry, Dad, I've got to go to practice now.

YOUR GRANDMOTHER: It's five A.M. Time to help me pull out the crabgrass before the dew melts.

YOU: Sorry, Grannie, I've got to go to practice now.

The idea is to make people believe that you do nothing but eat, sleep, and live sports. (Be careful. You know you've gone too far when your mother pops a Swanson's TV Basketball into the oven for your dinner.) Keep practicing these fundamentals until nuclear energy just sounds like something you get in the huddle and the Rolling Stones sounds like the description of a shot-put event. Once you've got this down, you're ready to move on.

# ★
# UNDER-
# STANDING
# THE JOCKS

Relax. This chapter does not have anything to do with forming a psychological comprehension of what it is to be an athlete, or anything so complex. This is a nuts-and-bolts lesson in how to figure out what the devil the jock is saying.

Fact of Life: At some time or another you will have to talk to an athlete and even appear to be engaged in conversation with him or her. Talking to other people as though you were a jock is one thing, but talking to an actual jock is something else—boy, is it something else!

But you'd never go into French, Spanish,

Latin, German, or Driver's Ed. without a dictionary, right? Well, we wouldn't let you tackle this next step in becoming a sports star unprepared, either.

# ★ DICTIONARY

## Jock-English

| What the Jock Says | What the Jock Means |
| --- | --- |
| Yo! | I am here; I am present. Used as response to someone calling jock's name. |
| Yo-Yo | It's not what you think and has nothing to do with the I.Q. of the jock. It means Siamese twin jocks are here. |
| He's an aggressive player. | He'd take a gun on the field if he didn't have to go through a metal detector first. |
| We let the coach down. | The coach chewed our ears off. |
| We let the school down. | The coach really chewed our ears off. |

| We let ourselves down. | A pack of wild rabbits chewed our ears off. |
|---|---|
| We're psyched up for this game. | I think I saw someone with a camera in the bleachers. |
| Winning isn't everything. | Why translate this? No one believes it. |
| We're not playing up to our ability. | If you guys don't shape up, I can kiss my pro career goodbye. |
| We played a good game. | I got to play a lot. |
| We were really clicking together like a well-oiled machine. | I got to play a lot. |
| Hey, Fox! How'd you like to go out with a star? | Hey, attractive person of the opposite sex! How would you like to go out with me? |
| They came to play. | Why did we let them get off the bus? |
| Coach Schmertz has taught me everything I know. | Both plays. |
| It was a defensive game. | Their defense figured out our two plays. |

| | |
|---|---|
| We'll get 'em next year. | Fortunately, I'll graduate so I won't have to take another beating like that. |
| A Star | A show-off |
| A Superstar | A show-off who breaks into commercials |
| A team player | Someone who can't show off |
| Most valuable player | Someone who gets on camera a lot |
| Wimps | Everyone else in the world |
| Home team advantage | We put something funny in their water. |
| Bump and Run | Pass play good for five to ten yards |
| Hit and Run | Good for ten to twenty years |
| Pigskin | A football |
| Pill | A baseball |
| Potato | A baseball |
| A Baseball | Scrambled eggs with a side of bacon |
| Playing dirty | If they get caught |
| Infraction of the rules | If we get caught |

# ★
# MAKING (UP)
# THE BIG PLAY

When telling stories about the big game in school, athletes have two objectives. The first is to make it seem as though they made game-winning contributions even though they may only have played briefly, if at all. The second objective is always ignored since the first is so important. And just because you're not on any team at all is no reason why you can't do the same.

This chapter will deal with three basic approaches to making (up) the big play: The Boorish Approach, The Fantastic Approach, and The Humble Approach. Of course, there are other approaches, some of which are too gruesome to be discussed in polite society, impolite society, or even this book. But by all means, experiment until you find the approach that best suits your personality and the gullibility of the people you're trying to fool.

# ★ THE BOORISH APPROACH

This consists of muscling your way into every conversation and telling long, drawn-out, self-important stories, so that no one can ever forget who's the star around here. This method requires a loud voice, a lot of breath, and a lot of nerve. It may seem unpleasant to you at first, but it's something that every athlete must learn.

Here is a sample speech illustrating The Boorish Approach. This example does not apply to all sports or situations, but since we went to a lot of trouble writing it, we expect you to read it attentively nevertheless.

**SAMPLE BOORISH SPEECH:**

Sure, maybe she did shoot the winning basket clear across court with only one second left in the game, but I'm the one who saved the day for the *whole school*. It happened like this. There were just a few seconds before halftime, and since I couldn't care less about what was happening in the game, I went out for some popcorn. That's when I discovered that they forgot to put any salt on it. Can you believe that? Well, I had to do some fast thinking. I knew if the popcorn wasn't salted, people wouldn't buy drinks. If they didn't buy drinks, the athletic department would lose money, and the school would look bad. Then the city would try to raise taxes again, but our parents would vote it down and the whole school system would have to be shut down. So I'm the one who told them to pour on the salt if they wanted to save our schools from economic collapse!

Perhaps you're asking yourself how can a stupid, egotistical, and obviously made-up story like that make you look like an athlete? Who else but an athlete would tell a story like that?! Get it? After a few weeks of excruciating stories, no one will be able to tell you from a real athlete. Trust us.

# ★ THE FANTASTIC APPROACH

Similar to the Boorish Approach, but not matching. The main difference is that instead of making your audience fall asleep you leave them wide awake and *speechless*.

## SAMPLE FANTASTIC REMARKS:

BASKETBALL STAR: Of course I timed my last shot perfectly so that I'd make the winning basket just as the clock ran out.

YOU: But you would have missed that shot by five feet if I hadn't used my mental powers and made the ball go through the hoop.

HOCKEY STAR: It was a one-in-a-million shot, but I knew if anyone could do it, I could.

YOU: That's because I was looking at the goalie's eyes and hypnotized him for a minute.

**or**

BROADJUMP STAR: I'd never jumped that far before, but I just couldn't let the rest of the team down.

YOU: It's a good thing I was there. Just when you took off, I inhaled deeply and the moving air currents made you go farther.

The beauty of this approach is that no one can really prove you're lying because of the possibility that it's all true. Stranger things have happened, especially in driver's education class. In no time at all, the word will get around school about your amazing contributions to the team, and people will start looking at you with new respect.

The Fantastic Approach works in your favor even when the team loses. You can claim that you were not at the game, which only strengthens your credibility. Or you can claim that your powers were undermined by a particular member of the team who, for some reason, didn't believe in you. This not only earns you sympathy, but it's also a chance to discredit someone on the team you don't especially like. But be careful. To succeed in sports without ever playing you must be accepted by the other athletes as well as the fans. (See "Getting Along with Real Players.")

# ★ THE HUMBLE APPROACH

Unlike the previous approaches, this one requires subtlety. The Humble Approach is the technique of always praising yourself while seeming never to talk about yourself.

## SAMPLE HUMBLE APPROACH

YOU: You've got to admit, the team is really improving. As I was telling Coach Schmertz—or "Schmertzie," as he keeps asking me to call him—those guys really picked up on every trick I taught them. When they get it all together, they'll be a team I could really be proud to play on.

If that speech were any more humble, you'd think it was a politician running for re-election. But let's examine the underlying messages in instant replay.

1) *"You've got to admit, the team is really improving."* This is a nice way of pointing out that even though the team is still losing 79–13, at least they're playing the second half and not forfeiting the way they used to. It makes you look big when you find something nice to say about these losers . . . an invaluable trait for a winning athlete.

2) *"As I was telling Coach Schmertz—or 'Schmertzie,' as he keeps asking me to call*

*him—*" Right away people will think that you are the coach's right-hand person, even though you're only a pain in his neck.

3) *"Those guys really picked up on every trick I taught them."* Last week they finally mastered using silverware, and next week they may even be ready for basketball.

4) *"When they get it all together . . . "* Stranger things have happened, especially in driver's education class.

5) *"They'll be a team I could really be proud to play on."* This remark clinches your total superiority as an athlete and, at the same time, makes you seem generous when you consent to play with these turkeys.

Once you've mastered these techniques of making (up) the big play, you can use them in your other classes. Imagine: "How I Ended World War II" or "How I Discovered a Mathematical Equivalent for Pi" or "Dinosaur Bones I Have Unearthed with the Help of My Dog"!

★

# FAKING
# IMPORTANT
# INJURIES

In the eyes of most people, an injured sports player is a cut (or a bruise) above the other players. As the famous sports psychologist, Harvey A. Heart, has pointed out on many occasions: "Show me a man or a woman who plays with pain, and I'll show you someone with a strange hobby." Oddly enough, Dr. Heart insisted for many years that that remark made sense.

An injury may be a medal of honor or a badge of courage to some, but to non-athletes it's just a pain in the neck. Unless you use it to your advantage!

# ★ THE IMPORTANCE OF BEING INJURED

Giving the appearance of being injured can be very beneficial, especially if you are following the premise of this book and not just looking at the pictures.

An injury shows that you are the kind of reckless and crazy player who will do anything for the team. This means people will admire you.

An injury shows that you are an intense and loyal player. This means even if your team is losing 62-zip before "The Star-Spangled Banner" is even played, you won't be blamed.

But most important, an injury means that people will open doors for you and give up their seats on crowded buses for you. It means you won't have to do calisthenics in phys. ed. right after lunch; you won't have to do your chores around the house. People will sympathize, pamper, and fawn over you from sunup to sundown.

In other words, an injured player has it made in the shade by getting all the glory without doing any of the work. So get out your crutches and Ace bandages and start deciding where you hurt the most!!

# ★ CHOOSING AN INJURY THAT'S RIGHT FOR YOU

Internal injuries — your basic bruised livers, kicked kidneys, ruptured spleens, collapsed lungs, and upset tummies — are not important injuries of any consequence. Why? Because they don't show. People have to see it to believe it. That's why a limp, a cane, a crutch, a cast, or a sling will mean more to you than any X ray. Here is a list of the most popular injuries associated with various sports, and some of their advantages.

*Baseball* — pitcher's elbow. Requires no strain. Written tests are therefore impossible.
*Field Hockey* — bruised knees. Cannot climb stairs to attend class.
*Soccer* — severe headaches. Avoid loud noises, such as teachers' and parents' lectures.
*Wrestling* — everyone knows that no one gets hurt, because wrestling is fixed, even in high school.
*Hockey* — sore throat from calling other team names. Cannot be expected to give answers in class.
*Football* — pulled hamstring. No one knows what a hamstring is so you can get away with everything from a wheelchair to eating ice cream in class.
*Musical Chairs* — pulled F-string.
*Swimming* — chlorinated tear ducts. Causes you to sob uncontrollably whenever you are

asked to change clothes for gym.

*Tennis* — tennis elbow. See *Baseball*, pitcher's elbow, above. Choose either sport depending on the style and value of your wardrobe and your ability to tolerate chewing tobacco.

*Racquetball* — bruised everything. Cannot pass through hallways with crowds. Must have additional twenty minutes between classes to assure no painful contact.

*Skiing* — broken everything. Cannot attend school at all. Important hint: Be sure to wrap every available limb in hundreds of yards of gauze bandages so that no one will have the energy to say, "Is that really broken? Let's see what you're hiding under that cast."

*Basketball* — temporary deafness from unbearable reverberations in the gym. Cannot hear own name when called on in class.

*Archery* — irreversible squint from looking at targets all day. Unable to focus on anything less than 50 yards away — textbooks, for instance.

*Bowling* — broken toes. Use your imagination to explain this one. Cannot participate in *any* other sports, but still mobile enough to attend movies with the cutest kid in school.

---
★
---

# EATING LIKE
# AN ATHLETE

Maybe you're thinking to yourself that this will be a short chapter comprised of one simple edict: "Take your hand and stuff food into your mouth. Repeat action." Wrong! That may be one way to get into the Book of World Records, but it does nothing to help you look like an athlete. (Note: This technique *is*, however, described in the "Special Section: Eating Like a Jock," later in this chapter.)

Athletes are very particular about where they eat and what they eat. And from now on, so will you be.

## ★ CHOOSING A SPOT TO EAT

When selecting a place to eat, most people

consider the quality of the food. After all, at today's prices you don't want to see something on your plate that has sickly green stripes and seems to inhale and exhale mysteriously under its own power. Yeeccch!

Other people consider the service when choosing anything from a restaurant to a fast burger joint. If the service is so slow that by the time you get your food it has sickly green stripes and seems to . . . etc., what have you gained?

Don't even bother answering that last question because quality of food and service are of no interest to someone who wants to seem like an athlete. You should concern yourself with this and only this consuming question: "Will I be seen?" Why do you want to be seen, you ask? Because you're not eating like an athlete for your *health*, after all. You're doing it to create an effect! Please keep in mind the secret of this book's success: It's not what you do but who sees you do it that counts.

So forget signs that say "Fine Food" or "Speedy Service" or "We haven't killed anyone yet . . . completely." Even if there are ten ambulances in the parking lot on call twenty-four hours a day, if a sign says, "Large Seating Capacity," any would-be athlete worth his or her weight in Gatorade will eat there.

# ★WHAT TO EAT

Contrary to everything anyone has said, or anything everyone has said, or even anything we've said, athletes do not eat anything (or everything) that does not move.

To be like them, you too (or you two if you are reading this book aloud to someone) will have to adopt a special diet depending on what sport you choose. The important thing, though, is to always make a big fuss about what you can and cannot eat. This announces the fact that people are dealing with a serious athlete.

# ★ DIETARY RULES:

- Football players do not eat pork, bacon, or sausages, since they spend so much time "eating the pigskin" during the game.

- Runners eat only fast foods.

- Basketball players avoid fowls.

- Cricket players eat frog legs.

- Frogmen eat soggy sandwiches unless they come to the surface first.

- Sharks eat frogmen.

- Tennis players will never accept fresh fish in a restaurant because it's a net serve.

- Wrestlers only eat in a price-fixed restaurant.

- Swimmers only eat in dives.

- Pitchers won't eat any fried shrimp because they can't face the heavy batter.

- Hockey players love a good stick-to-the-ribs meal.

- Coaches don't eat anything. Except they eat their hearts out.

# ★ SPECIAL SECTION: Eating Like a Jock

Not only will this section separate the men from the boys and the women from the girls, it may also separate the lunches from the stomachs. This section may be hard to swallow for sensitive readers. In other words, if you're really serious about looking like a jock, now's the time to put up or shut up and maybe throw up. Here are the rules:

## BE FEARLESS

Eat in the cafeteria. Most people go to the cafeteria because it's a good place to meet, talk to friends, and organize relay races with rodents of varying sizes. But jocks actually eat there.

A true jock eats rapidly. Open mouth; insert food (or facsimile; we won't even pretend it's reasonable); swallow; repeat. A true jock — and this is the hard part — never looks at his or her food. Perhaps in the past you enjoyed the luxury of going through your cafeteria food and separating the rubbery stuff from the rubbery stuff that moves. But no more. If it's on the plate, a jock will gobble it down and ask for seconds.

# TABLE MANNERS

Every jock knows what forks, knives, and spoons are used for — showing your strength by bending them into as many shapes as possible. Angie O'Graham, a senior known for her strong arms and nimble fingers, once bent a single knife and soup spoon into the shape of the entire Pledge of Allegiance.

Jocks, contrary to the stereotypical picture many people form about them, do not wipe their mouths on their shirtsleeves. Instead, they wipe their mouths on your shirtsleeves. If you notice that suddenly everyone around you is wearing short-sleeved clothes, you'll know that you're making progress and are beginning to eat like a jock.

Remember, jocks always say "Excuse me" when they belch loudly after their meals. Unfortunately, no one ever hears them because everyone generally leaves the cafeteria in disgust long before that.

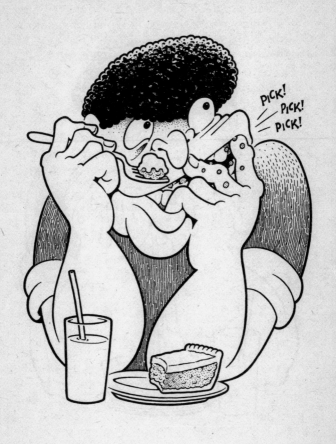

*Wrong* — eating with one hand in mouth

*Right* — eating with both hands in mouth

*Wrong* — sitting back after cleaning your plate

*Right* — eating from everyone else's plates

*Wrong* — jock spitting food as he talks incessantly to others at the table

*Right* — group of jocks all spitting food at each other as they talk incessantly while eating

# ★
# TWENTY OBSCURE FACTS TO END ANY SPORTS ARGUMENT

One other activity athletes and sports fans seem to find endlessly fun is testing each other's encyclopedic memory of sports information, statistics, and trivia. It's sort of the same thing as arm wrestling without the grunting.

Most athletes just try to get by remembering what sports reporters say on TV, but some players have been know to read one or maybe even two books to prepare for the challenge of one of these sports arguments.

You don't have to go to all of that trouble. In fact, you won't have to go to any trouble whatsoever. Below is a list of twenty obscure facts guaranteed to give you the last word in any sports argument. Because no athlete or sports fan will want to appear unknowledgeable, no one will ever challenge you. They will simply nod their heads and say weakly, "Oh, yeah. I forgot."

Go to it, champ!

1) The 1947 Kentucky Derby winner was disqualified when it was discovered that the jockey was a cocker spaniel.

2) The old Washington "Red Faces" was the first team to play an overtime game in the dark and lose.

3) The basketball hoop is not really round, but nobody cares.

4) The difference between American football and Canadian football is that American players are chosen in the draft and Canadian players avoid it.

5) The 1948, the Olympic Long Jump Gold medalist was disqualified when it was discovered he was a cocker spaniel, previously disqualified from the high hurdle event.

6) Rugby, the most vicious sport of all, has been banned from every swimming pool in the English-speaking world.

7) The game of squash is not named after the vegetable, squash. It is named after the carrot.

8) No woman has ever gotten lost at the Astrodome.

9) Billy Martin was fired from the New York Yankees when it was discovered that he might be a cocker spaniel.

10) One quarterback played the entire 1962 football season without a helmet and earned the nickname "Jerk."

11) Badminton used to be played with real birds.

12) There actually was one retired pro football player who did not go into broadcasting.

13) Upton D. Rufus was the first man to sell hot dogs at a baseball game, and yet he died penniless. He tried selling them to the players.

14) Les Izmore tried out for mascot of the North Southern University rowing team, but he was disqualified when it was discovered he wasn't a cocker spaniel.

15) The world pole-vault record was broken three times by a man who says he did it when no one was looking.

16) Ethel Enalbert, an Olympic javelin thrower, broke the *standing broadjump* record by forgetting to let go of the javelin.

17) Jeff Boyardi has run in every marathon in every major city in the United States and has never finished a race.

18) When men challenge women in doubles tennis, women wear skirts three times more often them men.

19) Swimming is the only sport that doesn't exercise your tongue.

20) The world chess champion once played 243 simultaneous games of chess while his hotel room was being robbed.

# ★
# GETTING ALONG WITH <u>REAL</u> PLAYERS

By now you know how to look like an athlete and how to talk like one. But before you start planning your own line of sports equipment, clothes, and shoe laces, you've got to put yourself to the true test. Namely: Can You Fool the Real Athletes?

Of course you can! How? you ask. Well, for one thing you can stop asking so many questions and breaking up the flow of the writing style.

To get along with real athletes you are going to have to develop precision athletic behavior.

Research tells us that athletes behave one way in public—very physical. But they behave another way when they're in the privacy of their own company—more physical.

Athletes lives are filled with special rituals and gestures that set them apart from the rest of us, although a high brick wall would work just as well. Nevertheless, your success in this whole charade depends on making those rituals and gestures as much a part of your life as combing your hair and scrubbing your tongue.

Here are some things to watch for and watch out for as you mingle with the real athletes.

# ★ HAND JIVE

Athletes do a lot of talking with their hands. Sometimes you'll find athletes who talk *to* their hands, but only very strange and lonely athletes.

Athletes have special hand gestures to say almost everything—"Hello"; "Congratulations"; "Better luck next time"; "Go get 'em"; and "Excuse me, but what's the proper way to tie an ascot?" Unfortunately, all the gestures have one thing in common—they all hurt.

A typical athlete greeting includes a bone-breaking handshake, several more hip "street" handshakes, slapping five, a thump on the back, a slap on the bottom, a pat on the head, and a pinch of oregano if the athlete is saying hello to a pizza.

Recently two athletes were greeting each other in the aforementioned manner, and they attracted a large crowd of hopeful drama students who mistook the scene for an audition for *The Miracle Worker*.

Why do athletes continually slap, pound, and push each other? Some experts believe it's the expression of camaraderie; others attribute it to hostility. Experts, shmexperts! The truth is they've got hands, and they have to break something. That's why they're athletes, not pastry chefs.

**Tips to Remember:**
- Slap Me Five does not mean "Slap me five times."
- Always remove the bat or racket from your hand before slapping your teammates' bottoms. That's the major difference between sports and a brawl.
- Never scream in agony when in the viselike handshake of an athlete. It's a sign of weakness.
- Never shake hands with the same athlete twice. It's a sign of stupidity. A slap on the bottom or a chair over the head is an acceptable alternative greeting.
- Special Note to Football Players: Never let a teammate pound on your shoulders to test your shoulder pads—you don't have any.

# ★ SUPERSTITIOUS MINDS

Many athletes credit their success to dumb

luck; and they're probably half right. It's hard to find a more superstitious group than athletes without venturing back to Salem, Massachusetts, in the good old days.

If athletes have a good day, they believe something they did caused them to have good luck. The only catch is they don't know exactly what that something was. So as not to take any chances, they have to do everything, eat everything, wear everything the same every time they play. Some pro players have been living the same day in 1955 over and over for more than twenty-five years. Talk about a time warp.

Speaking of being a little warped, these are some of the common sports superstitions you should know and use when in the company of real athletes.

- It's unlucky if you find the coach tied up in the shower.
- In a baseball dugout, it's unlucky to use the words *no-hitter, perfect game,* and *conifer.*
- It's unlucky to play an away game when the rest of the team is playing at home.
- Teddy bears, hamburgers with thirteen pickles, spitting in your hands are good luck (unless you're holding the hamburger at the time). Reversible jackets, anyone named "Lucky," laughing when the coach swallows a whistle are bad luck.
- Changing clothes in the middle of a game is good luck; changing clothes in the middle of the field is bad luck.

- Surprisingly enough, wearing someone else's shoes can be good luck, but not while they're wearing them.
- It's bad luck if the other team brings baseball bats to a football game.
- The best luck is when you find a worm in your sandwich, after you've already given someone else the first bite.

# ★ THE NAME GAME

All athletes have nicknames. This means you'd better decide on one for yourself. That way, if you forget the handshakes and the superstitions, you'll at least have a convincing sports nickname to cover yourself with the real jocks.

Nicknames come from three sources: what you look like, what you act like, and what your name really is.

1) You're probably used to your friends calling you such gems as Bird Legs, Four-Eyes, Putty Nose, and Zits Haven. But athletes have a way of zeroing in on a physical attribute and then coming up with an affectionate nickname, like Bird Legs, Four-Eyes, Putty Nose, and Zits Haven. No one said athletes were any kinder than your friends.

2) Sometimes athletes acquire their nicknames after a special and memorable feat. A nickname such as Bone-Crusher, Angel of Death, or Flunk-Out reflects what you can do best.

3) The nickname that connotes the most re-

spect and affection in sports is one derived from one's own name. Baseball's Carl Yastremski is called "Yaz," football's John Matuzak is called "Tooz," and tennis star Anthea Kosimaddenadous is called "Brainless" because she always forgets her racket.

In case your name doesn't lend itself to the short form—or has unfortunate connotations, as in Bob Brown being called "Brownie"—here is a random list of nicknames that you can easily adopt as your own. Simply see a lawyer about the adoption papers.

> "Long Arm"
> "Muscle Teeth"
> "Big Legs"
> "Very Big Legs"
> "Rump Roast"
> "Bench Buddy"
> "The Jumper"
> "Ran Halfway Down the Field and Scored Real Big"
> "Rambler"
> "Vince Lombardi"
> "Hands of Gold"
> "Heart of Gold"
> "Wallet of Gold"
> "Gone with the Wind"
> "Star Wars"

# ★
# THREE RULES IF YOU WANT TO BE A CHEERLEADER

**RULE #1:** Throw this book away. Cheerleaders are not athletes and they do not need to know anything at all about sports. Cheerleaders are merely ordinary people with hyperactive thyroid problems.

**RULE #2:** Don't try to fake it. Unlike real sports, you can never convince anyone that you are a cheerleader without screaming a lot, bouncing around in utter excitement at every opportunity, and demonstrating a sincere compulsion to form human pyramids.

**RULE #3:** Be sure to shave your legs, even if you are a boy. It is part of the cheerleaders' credo.

★

# FIFTEEN USABLE FACE-SAVING REASONS WHY YOU DIDN'T MAKE THE TEAM

Not everyone can make the team. If you use this book as a guide and play your cards right, you should be one of the lucky ones who doesn't. But does that mean that you have to go back to being the uncoordinated loser you were before you bought this life-changing book? When everyone hears why you were cut, you'll be a bigger hero than ever!

1) Your hair clashes with the uniform, and you thought it would be bad for school spirit to have them change the colors.

2) Everyone is smaller than you are, and it wouldn't be fair to play against them.

3) Everyone is much larger than you are, and it wouldn't be fair to their consciences if they were always worried about killing you.

4) You and the coach disagreed on your assignments. (He wanted you to play defense; you wanted to sit on the bench.)

5) Sports would keep you from your serious studying. (And you've already got twenty things keeping you from studying.)

6) Your religious beliefs prohibit you from wearing sweat socks.

7) Every team has to have a star, but why should you hog all of the attention?

8) You've already had three offers from the pros. Why risk injuring yourself?

9) The team was not playing hard enough because they depended entirely on you.

10) The principal told you about big changes in the athletics program, which you're not allowed to reveal.

11) You gave up baseball to take a job in a coal mine so that your contributions to charity would be bigger this year.

12) Fourteen pro hockey players sent you a letter begging you not to play until they retired.

13) You were so good they decided to retire your number even before you played.

14) You've already donated your body to science, and you want it to be in good condition when it gets there.

15) The coach is afraid he won't have anything to do because your leadership qualities are so strong.

# ★
# HOW TO AVOID PLAYING IF YOU ACCIDENTALLY <u>DO</u> MAKE THE TEAM

Stranger things have happened, especially in driver's education class. What does it mean if you do make the team? Well, it means that you've succeeded in making everyone, including the coach, think that you are a star athlete. And that means our mission is completed.

But if, after following the book's directions, you're left in the lurch and right in the soup, try these methods of bowing out gracefully without getting the boot when you do.

# ★ THE DISCOURAGING WORD APPROACH

What's the worst thing you can do when playing on a team? Sell your plays to the opposing team? Sell your teammates to the opposing team? Kill one of the officials? Small potatoes compared to the Number One unforgivable sin of LOSING TEAM SPIRIT. With this small yet powerful weapon, you can get under the coach's skin faster than an army of kamakazi mosquitoes. All you have to do is casually drop a negative and discouraging word at the crucial time—right before the coach sends you in to play. For example, mutter to yourself:

"I don't know why he's sending me in. We're going to lose this game anyway."

**or**

"I'm only going to play at 50% today so I'll be ready for a game that really counts."

**or**

"Maybe I'll huddle with the other team. They've got all the good plays."

**or**

"Maybe they should change the school colors to black and blue."

Remarks like these are guaranteed to send you to the showers and your coach to a home for excitable people who need to be watched closely. But is there really a choice when it comes down to you having to play? Well, yes there is. You can always try:

# ★ THE AMNESIAC APPROACH

Okay, maybe this was a little hokey even when they tried it in old movies. But we're talking about the bruises and contusions your body and reputation will suffer if you are forced to set foot on the playing field.

To pull this off, you will have to be very, very convincing and believable. Think believable when you sit on the other team's bench and go into their locker room. Or when you call the coach by the wrong name or when you face the net backwards or put your shoes on the wrong foot (put them on someone else's feet if possible).

The coach will have no choice except to believe that you were injured in practice, and he'll keep you out of the game to avoid controversy and a lawsuit.

Don't forget the other advantages of the Amnesiac Approach. When used in a regular classroom, where you stare vacantly into space or point at pretty pictures of kitty cats in books, your teachers will be more convinced than ever that you are a 100% genuine athlete.

# ★ THE BROKEN EQUIPMENT APPROACH

Obviously, you can't be sent in to play if you have equipment or uniform problems. Or, as Coach Pop "Lameduck" Schmertz always told reporters, "You show me a player without his uniform, and I'll show you someone who is going to get arrested real soon," even though no one ever asked him.

Nevertheless, here's a handy checklist of items you'll need at all times. Select the ones that are appropriate to the sport you're avoiding and to your budget.

- One pair of shoelaces broken in two places so they cannot be tied back together.

- One uniform jersey or shirt ripped to shreds. Explanation: You must have kept it in the drier too long.
  (Incidentally, if you have a coach who is a fanatic about clean uniforms, a shirt with a bad chocolate stain should be enough to send you to the showers or dry cleaners for weeks.)

- Three pairs of eyeglasses, cracked.

- Basketball or track shoes with metal taps

- Papier-mâché mouthpiece.

- Pre-soaked sweatbands.

- One pair of mittens instead of handball, golf, or bowling gloves.

- A large bottle of calamine lotion—never underestimate the potent threat of a roaring case of poison ivy.

- Face guard with no eye holes.

You're probably scratching your head and wondering to yourself how in the world we could have omitted the greatest stalling device since the gasoline engine. Of course, we mean the contact lens. Well, maybe you should be wondering how silly you look sitting there scratching your head—ever think of that, know-it-all? We've devoted an entire section to:

# ★ THE CARE AND LOSING OF CONTACT LENSES

The contact lens, as you may have heard, is the greatest stalling device since the gasoline engine, a joke that doesn't seem to get funnier in the retelling, but we'll keep trying.

Thanks to modern technology, contact lenses, especially the new soft, plastic ones, have become much easier and quicker to put in and take out. But don't let this discourage you. With a little practice you'll learn to become so clumsy and inept with your lenses that you'll be able to stall for another ten precious minutes of sitting on the bench if the coach tries to send you into the game.

But what if the coach sends you in early in the game? It's not likely that you can stall the entire game, spilling cleaning liquids, poking yourself in the eye, nearly swallowing your contact lenses. Don't lose your cool; lose your contact lens, preferably right in the middle of the playing field or court. The simple statement "I've lost my contact lens" can bring anything—sports events, tests, traffic, possibly even wars—to a complete standstill. After several minutes of watching athletes crawl around on their hands and knees looking for a contact lens instead of slamming their bodies together in contact sports, audiences will start to boo restlessly, and your coach will make an immediate substitution for you. At this point, don't forget to be escorted from the field in your near-blind condition. It's a nice touch. Being carried off on a stretcher is going a bit too far, though.

For those of you on a tight budget, we recognize that contact lenses are a large investment and possibly more than you bargained for when you set out to fool people into thinking you're an athlete. This next example is for you.

Sherman Oaks of California was sent in to pinch-hit late in the season by his coach. Sherman started putting in his contact lenses and twenty minutes later, trotted to home plate. Immediately he fell on his hands and knees. At first the umpire thought Sherman was praying for a hit, but soon he called a time-out while everyone searched for Sherman's missing contact lens. Sherman was able to delay the game for a world record fourteen days, at which time he graduated and never did have to take his turn at bat.

But more important than that: Sherman Oaks has perfect eyesight and doesn't even wear glasses! So who said anything about *buying* contact lenses?

## ★ THE INJURED PLAYER APPROACH

See "Faking Important Injuries." If it can work on your schoolmates, it can work on your coach.

## ★ OTHER APPROACHES

Once in a while, you're going to confront a really hard-nosed coach who will try to send you into a game and won't take no for an answer. You'll try the Discouraging Word Approach, and he'll tape your mouth closed and send you into the game anyway. You'll try the Amnesiac Approach, and he'll say it doesn't matter if you can't remember the plays—just get out there and bleed. You'll try the Broken Equipment Approach and the Lost Contact Lens trick, and he'll give you a seeing-eye dog and send you into the game anyway.

What do you do when all else fails? Try the

**BEGGING APPROACH.** Make it simple. Avoid questions like "Why me?" or "Why don't you send in one of the cheerleaders?" Stick to the basics, like "Please!" and "I'll do anything, just don't send me in there!"

Sure it's embarrassing, but desperate people will do desperate things.

---
★
---

# FIFTEEN THINGS THAT CAN GIVE YOU AWAY

BEWARE! No matter how carefully you follow our plans, these fifteen pitfalls are around every corner. Avoid them at all costs.

- Trying to pay for your free throws.
- Saying you read about a game in the newspaper. You either saw the game on TV or you were there.
- Studying (even for a test) the night before a match or game.
- Not knowing who Vince Lombardi is, especially if you're a distant relative.

- Asking to see a cartoon before the game films.
- Asking to see a cartoon *instead* of the game films.
- Uttering the phrase "It's only a game."
- Not standing for the school alma mater, the school fight song, or the school bus.
- Carrying your books in an attaché case.
- Not holding hands in the huddle.
- Holding hands in the locker room.
- Uttering the phrase "Hope we get lucky today."
- Applying for an athletic scholarship to medical school.
- Not allowing the school newspaper photographer to take your picture when you're all sweaty.
- Missing the Athletic Dinner, even for a great date.

# WHEN ALL ELSE FAILS . . .

We'll be the last to admit it — that's why we've saved it for the last chapter — but this system isn't 100% foolproof. It all depends on how many fools there are in your school. It's possible that someone could come up to you and say, "I was at the track meet yesterday. I thought you said you could pole-vault without a pole." Or "I'm on the basketball team and you haven't even been to one of the practices." Or "This is a stick-up. Give me your watch and wallet." Well, you're going to need some answers pretty fast and a new watch and wallet soon after. And we've got 'em —

the answers, that is. All you need to do is announce that you've switched to a new sport. Don't worry — no one will challenge you on any of the details because no one has ever *heard* of these athletic atrocities. These are sports that boggle the imagination and defy description.

## DONKEY TENNIS

A variation on the traditional Donkey Basketball where players play a game of basketball while riding donkeys. This is a favorite of everyone except the janitors who clean up the gym.

## DONKEY HORSESHOES

See above.

## DONKEY PIN-THE-TAIL-ON-THE-DONKEY

See a doctor.

## 120-METER CHAIR RACE

Not to be confused with a chariot race. Twelve shoeless players run a 120-meter course of hurdles, hazards, and highway patrol radar units while carrying folding beach chairs high over their heads. This game is derived from an ancient sports event popular during the Italian Beach Chair Famine of 1516, when players' houses were being ripped off during a tidal wave.

## PHYSICAL PUNISHMENT

Usually the name of this game alone is enough to frighten off any skeptic's questions. It is the most grueling sport in the world. Two teams of ten players each line up on a rocky, litter-filled field facing each other. Players then tackle, shove, block, elbow, push, stomp, crush, and maul each other until the game is over. Since there is no ball or goal line, no one ever scores. In fact, few survive the season, especially if it goes into overtime. This game is obviously for the true believer of the axiom: "It isn't whether you win or lose, but how you play the game."

## CIRCULAR RACE

This is a tricky and not often heard of game that involves agility, quick responses, as well as auditory acuity. Seven players circumnavigate the perimeter of a row of six chairs, aligned in a single column, no less than three inches apart. The event is accompanied by the popular mode of music indigenous to the host country. When an interruption in the musical performance occurs, all players must spring into the second phase of play, instantaneously selecting and claiming as their own "territory" one of the chairs in the column. Players who are left standing without "territory" are disqualified from the event. Play can only continue after the field is diminished by one chair. (If they buy all that, feel free to tell them you made the varsity squad when you were a freshman.)

## INDIA WRESTLING

Not to be confused with Indian wrestling. Opponents assume full lotus position facing each other; then they begin to meditate. They imagine they are like water washing over a rock; they see themselves as one with the pickle in the lettuce, cheese, onions, and special sauce on a sesame seed bun. Winner is the first player to lose his grip on total reality and still be able to uncross his legs.

## ROLLER BOWLER

At speeds of up to 51 miles per hour (and often in 20 mph zones) roller-skating daredevils hurl themselves flat on their bellies down bowling alleys toward ten pins that have been Krazy-Glued to the floor when the skaters were not looking. Players believe that performing a crazy stunt like this is the fastest way of getting on a popular television series — *M\*A\*S\*H*.

## GIVE THEM ENOUGH ROPE TUG-OF-WAR

Traditional game of muscle and endurance played in an untraditional setting. Both teams stand in pools of quicksand. No team has ever been presented the national trophy, and it's just as well because no one ever bothered to buy one.

## THE MEGA-DECATHALON

The ultimate in the thrill of victory and the agony of defeat. Players compete simultaneously in barefoot logrolling, cobweb cat's cradle, bed-of-nails surfing, shot-put juggling, greased pig kissing, rum-running, underwater paddleball, knitting needle rhyming, meringue soccer, and space invaders. First player to think of a good reason for this wins.

## SPORTS REPORTING

When all else *really* fails, you can claim that you're no longer an athlete but you've gone on to sports journalism and now all you do is talk about athletes, make fun of them, dig into their indiosyncracies, and put down their every move — in other words, everything this book has taught you to do. Well, *that's* not very nice! That's not nice at all! So you'd better apologize. After all, if it weren't for gym class, you'd be stuck taking Music Appreciation five times a week instead of two! Now aren't you sorry? (By the way, if this really happens to you, see our new book *How to Succeed at Music Appreciation without Ever Listening.*)